GROWING UP
IN THE OLD WEST

JUDITH ALTER
GROWING UP
IN THE OLD WEST

WITHDRAWN

Franklin Watts
New York / London / Toronto / Sydney
A First Book / 1989

Cover photograph courtesy of The Granger Collection

Photographs courtesy of: The Granger Collection:
pp. 6, 10 (both), 12, 15 (bottom), 17 (both), 27,
29, 45, 50 (top), 54, 58; Kansas State Historical
Society, Topeka: pp. 11, 22, 33 (both), 35, 57;
Bettmann Archive: pp. 13, 15 (top), 38, 39, 40,
43, 46, 50 (bottom), 53, 56; New York Public Library
Picture Collection: pp. 19, 25, 30, 37 (both).

Library of Congress Cataloging-in-Publication Data

Alter, Judy, 1938–
Growing up in the Old West / Judith Alter.
p.   cm.—(A First book)
Bibliography: p.
Includes index.
Summary: Describes the hardships, threats, chores, games,
amusements, and challenges that made growing up in the Old West a
dangerous but exciting experience.
ISBN 0-531-10746-9
1. Frontier and pioneer life—West (U.S.)—Juvenile literature.
2. Children—West (U.S.)—Juvenile literature. [1. Frontier and
pioneer life—West (U.S.)   2. West (U.S.)—Social life and customs.]
I. Title.   II. Series.
F591.A34   1989
978—dc19   88-34547 CIP AC

CONTENTS

INTRODUCTION

What was it like to grow up in the Old West—the time roughly between the 1840s and the 1890s? All wild adventure and excitement? Days and days in a covered wagon crossing the prairie and always watching for Indians; or living on a ranch and learning to ride at the age of two, carry a gun at eight, and herd cattle at ten? Or was it really long, dull days with little to do and nothing to eat but cornbread? In truth, it was all those things.

Sometimes youngsters worked from dawn to dark, coaxing crops out of a stubborn soil and helping to make everything the family needed, from food and clothes to furniture. But there were glorious good times too—days spent hunting, fishing, or exploring the prairie; wonderful community gatherings that brought friends and gaiety into ordinarily lonely lives; high jinks that might be as dangerous as they were exciting. And Indians and outlaws were not just the stuff of stories; too often they were a real and daily presence growing up on the frontier.

The real Old West was not just one time or one place. Geographically, it ranged from the rainy forests of the Northwest to the dry, desertlike land of what is now New Mexico and Arizona; from the endless flat prairies of Kansas and Nebraska to the jagged Rocky Mountains of Texas and Montana.

HOME IS
WHERE THE HEART IS

"Wagons Ho!" The first wagon trains to roll West under the traditional wagonmaster's cry left Missouri in the early 1840s. For the children on a wagon train, the wagon itself became the only home they had for at least six months. Settlers went West in almost anything with wheels, from farm wagons to the so-called prairie schooner, or covered wagon.

The wagon bed of the prairie schooner was generally about ten feet long by four feet wide, not much bigger than a double bed. In that space, families carried not only what was essential for the trip, but also what was necessary to set up housekeeping at the end of the trail: bedding, supplies, cooking utensils, clothing, and lots of other things.

Outside the wagon hung tools and extra equipment, from chains and axles to hoes, plows, and shovels. A pair of oxen, wearing a heavy wooden yoke or collar, generally pulled the wagon, and

On the Road

Covered wagons became home to families crossing the wilderness—sometimes for as long as six months. The wagons were often overstuffed with an entire household's belongings, containing supplies for the journey west and to set up a new home.

A man with a whip in hand usually led the team pulling their precious cargo west. Facing page: Dancing, singing, and music provided some entertainment during the long journey west.

someone with a goad in hand had to walk alongside. That was usually man's work because it was hot and dirty and men generally handled livestock, but many women drove teams across the prairie, and sometimes the job fell to a young boy. Almost everyone else walked beside the wagon. Only the very old, the very young, and the ill rode.

The wagons rolled early in the morning. The day began at 4 A.M., but it was 6 or 7 A.M. before the train got under way. It took that long for the women and girls to cook breakfast and the men and boys to round up and hitch the teams. The train stopped long enough at noon for the animals to rest and the people to eat, then marched on until late afternoon. In the evening, weary settlers had a campfire supper, perhaps buffalo steak if the hunting had been good, with fried cakes—a mixture of flour and water cooked in beef or buffalo fat—or johnnycake made with cornmeal, buttermilk, and molasses. Dried apple pie was an occasional treat. After supper there might be dancing to a fiddle or perhaps music from a flute, but everyone turned in early.

Day after endless long day, they pushed on in the sun, heat, wind, and rain. As the train moved westward, both animals and people tired. Oxen sometimes dropped in their tracks and had to be cut out of their yokes. Fortunate families then hitched up one of the spare oxen or cattle trailing their wagon; others tried to continue with one animal. Increasingly, loads were lightened. Treasures that could not be parted with in Missouri were sadly abandoned less than a third of the way into the journey as families discovered how difficult the trip was and as they learned what was a necessity and what was a luxury.

The trail was also clearly marked by graves, sometimes so numerous they formed a border along the roughly rutted path. Movies and paintings have led us to believe that Indians posed a constant threat to wagon trains. In truth, Indians were far less a threat than accidental shootings and disease.

The land the pioneers crossed presented as many dangers as disease did. There were swollen and flooding rivers to cross. There were steep mountains to cross. Some roads hung dangerously over the edges of cliffs; others were extremely steep. Children were sometimes caught in stampedes and trampled by oxen hooves or they fell out of their wagons, in which case the wheels might crush them.

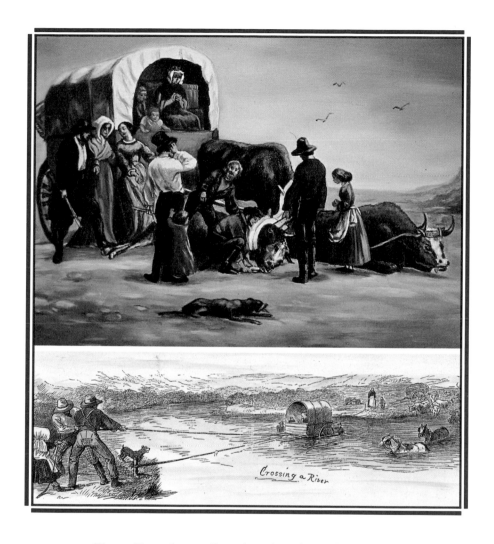

Top: People and animals often fell victim
to disease and exhaustion. Bottom: Crossing
steep mountains and wide rivers were among
the many difficulties pioneers faced.

Those first families to travel West were headed for Oregon and northern California; those that went later often traveled to warmer climates, perhaps Texas, where the weather made it possible for the wagon to serve as home for as long as six months to a year after the arrival at a homestead site. The family ate, slept, worked, and played outside the wagon.

But for those early families in the North, a permanent home had to be built immediately, before winter came. In that land of thick forests, they built log cabins. It took weeks to prepare to build such a house; the actual building sometimes took only a day, with neighbors all pitching in.

The classic house of the prairie was the sod hut, or soddy, as it was affectionately called. Each spring the grasses on the prairie greened, and each winter they died back, only to green again in the spring. Each new growth interlocked its roots with those already tangled in the soil, so that the earth itself was matted forever with a thick carpet of roots. This sod proved to be an unusual and ideal building material in a land where there were few trees.

The sod was cut from the earth in large blocks. The sod blocks were stacked, grass side down, in a staggered, overlapping pattern, much as bricks were used back East. The result was a thick and heavy wall, its cracks plastered with mud. A roof

Right: Children and neighbors helped clear the land, gather logs, and build homes.

Below: Some houses were built of sod blocks which kept cool in summer and warm in winter.

was built of crisscrossed willow or cottonwood poles and topped with brush or grass and a final layer of sod. It took one acre of sod to build a one-room house measuring only sixteen by twenty feet—about the size of a comfortable living room today—and the house likely weighed several tons. Inside, the walls were whitewashed. Floors were hard-packed dirt that had to always be swept to keep the dust down.

A sod house had its advantages. Because of the thick walls, a soddy was warm and snug in winter and tended to stay cool in the summer; it was fire-proof; it was cheap. But many settlers found the disadvantages discouraging. A soddy was always damp and musty; it was very dark inside and very small; dirt and sometimes little creatures—bugs and rodents—dropped down out of the ceiling. House-wives learned to drape cheesecloth beneath the rafters to catch the falling debris and to protect open food. In a heavy rain, water seeped through the roof, and it was impossible to find enough pails to catch every drip. Children were usually charged with catching drips and protecting bedding from a thorough soaking.

Furniture in many frontier homes was rough. Many families gathered around a crudely built wooden table, called a trestle table, for their meals,

Prairie homes were often
furnished with handmade tables,
chairs, beds, and benches.

but in some parts of the West even the planks to build a trestle table were expensive because of scarcity of timber.

Sometimes a bed had interwoven ropes to support a mattress, and frequently the mattress, such as it was, was a casing stuffed with dried grass. Clothing might be kept in crudely built open shelves, probably covered with a curtain, and chairs might be only as finely made as the carpentry skills of the man of the house would allow. Beyond the necessities—table and benches, a few chairs, a bed, somewhere to store clothes and dishes—there was not much furniture in a frontier home unless some, miraculously, survived the journey.

WORK FOR THE NIGHT IS COMING

Although a permanent home represented a big improvement over a wagon, life was still difficult. Daily living involved many chores unknown to us today. In some cases, those chores fell to youngsters.

Take, for instance, the problem of keeping the house supplied with water. Water had to be hauled from the nearest source—a spring or creek—until the homesteader could dig a well. Many a frontier youngster learned the lesson early on that it is easier to carry two buckets of water, one in each hand for balance, than to struggle along, lopsided, with one bucket. Sometimes a clever parent would fashion a leather yoke, much like the wooden ones used on oxen, with buckets hung from each end. The yoke fit over a child's shoulder, made hauling water easier, and probably lessened the chance of accidental spills.

*Water was precious on the frontier
and had to be carried into the house
from a well or nearby creek.*

Whether water was hauled from creek or well, it was treated like precious gold. The dishwater went to the chickens, any bathwater was poured on a struggling flowerbed or maybe a tree that the family was trying to coax into growing. To use water once and discard it carelessly was not to be thought of.

Hot water was available only when it was heated on the stove, and the Saturday night bath is probably not just a joke. Because of the scarcity of water and the difficulty in heating it, bathing was not the everyday thing we know today. When they did bathe, settlers used the same round tub that clothes were washed in, and probably the whole family used the same bathwater.

Washing clothes was not an easy chore either. Again, water had to be heated over a fire built outside with a wash pot suspended over it. Clothes were then put into the tub, along with homemade lye soap. A stick was used to push and poke at the clothes, doing the job of the cycle on today's washing machine that churns the clothes about in soapy water. Children often had to stand for endless hours poking that stick into a boiling kettle of laundry. Clothes were also rubbed on a washboard or pounded on a battling bench with a paddle-shaped board. This was a good way to beat the dirt out of men's trousers and work pants, but it required strength, and the job often fell to a man or young boy. Then clothes usually had to be put by hand through two or three rinses to remove the soap; hand-wringing clothes and bedding takes a surprising amount of strength.

Finally, clothes were spread on the prairie to dry. In winter, clothes froze solid and stiff before they dried, and in spring, they might be whipped to shreds in a storm. In parts of the West, housewives quickly learned to get wet clothes into the house before a dust- or hailstorm.

There was no indoor plumbing at this time. Surprisingly, pictures of sod huts on the prairie show the huts in lonely isolation, with no outhouse visible. In such cases, settlers probably used a nearby clump of trees for the privacy to relieve themselves, and at night a slop jar or chamber pot

Washing clothes was a major physical chore. After clothes were soaked in heated water, women often had to "pound" the dirt out.

was used. That added another chore for either the housewife or an unfortunate child—the slop jar had to be emptied and cleaned daily.

Washing, cooking, and the use of indoor plumbing are dependent on water and become difficult when water is not readily available. Similarly, a lot of everyday living is dependent on good lighting, an impossibility in frontier homes, where windows were often nothing more than holes in the wall covered by heavy wooden shutters unless the weather was particularly pleasant. Glass windows were late to come to the frontier. The earliest lamps on the frontier were open flat dishes, much like soup bowls, half filled with sand and then covered in coal oil. A nail or stick, embedded in the bottom of the dish or cup, anchored a wick, usually an old rag. Lighted, the wick gave off a faint light, surely not enough to read by.

Kerosene lamps brought a big improvement toward the end of the century. These lamps, probably familiar from pictures, had dish-like bases that held the kerosene, wicks that burned, and glass chimneys that controlled the flame. But here was another chore for children: the glass chimneys got smoky, especially if the flame was allowed to burn too high, and had to be cleaned; wicks scorched easily if the flame was not controlled and, scorched or not, had to be trimmed periodically.

Small children on the frontier
homestead helped by gathering twigs
and caring for small animals.

Collecting fuel for cooking and heating usually
fell on the children's chore list. Where wood was
plentiful, it was burned, and youngsters chopped
and stacked firewood. They also collected twigs,
grass, and hay to burn. Some stoves burned dried
corncobs or sunflower stalks.

But the primary fuel of the American prairie
was the cow pattie or buffalo chip. The droppings
of these animals, left to harden in the prairie sun,

made a satisfactory fuel. Many frontier women, at first loath to pick up the chips, soon learned to chuck them into a wheelbarrow or an upturned apron without a thought, having long since abandoned the gloves that at first protected their hands.

Youngsters' chores on the frontier tended to be divided into those done by boys and those done by girls, just as the work done by men and women was clearly defined and separate. Men, being thought stronger, handled the livestock and the outdoor chores, such as plowing and planting, and hunting. Running the house was the responsibility of the women, which especially without modern conveniences, was pure hard work. When possible, boys inherited the chores involved with the care of animals. Girls might milk a cow or a goat, but boys generally took care of the livestock.

In cattle country, boys learned early to handle horses, and most boys could sit a saddle by the time they were five or six. Even young boys were sent on errands on horseback or to inspect a water hole. Boys also learned to handle a horse team of two or four horses, and young boys could drive a team hitched to a plow or a wagon.

Girls generally were given the household chores—dipping candles, sewing, milking, baking bread, washing clothes. Taking care of younger children was an important responsibility for girls.

Frontiersmen plowed the fields and planted the crops, while women were responsible for running the house. Both these tasks were hard work.

But they also collected wood and buffalo chips, herded livestock, dug weeds, fed chickens and collected eggs, churned butter, made soap, and helped butcher hogs.

Sewing and cooking were probably the two chores that kept girls—and their mothers—the busiest. For meat, most families ate what the men could kill—deer, antelope, buffalo, prairie chickens, wild turkey, wild hogs. Some families butch-

ered their own hogs and cattle for the family table, particularly in the northern climates, where the meat could be hung in a shed all winter without spoiling, with pieces cut off as needed. Vegetables were grown and picked.

Standard supplies were often rare. Yeast might not be available to make bread rise, so a family ate soda bread or the now-famous sourdough—if the woman of the house kept a sourdough starter on the back of her stove. More likely, white flour was not available either, so the people ate cornbread in one form or another. A settler could raise and grind his own cornmeal using a mill, much like a big coffee grinder, that was nailed to a tree.

Sugar was brown, not the fine white product we're used to today, and coffee was a treat. If a housewife could get coffee, she likely had to roast and grind the beans. Dried beans and rice, easily stored, were bought in great quantities. Dried fruit could also be purchased in quantity and used to make pies for special occasions.

Cooking was one chore that kept prairie women very busy.

INNOCENT FUN AND DANGEROUS HIGH JINKS

Life on the frontier was hard work. There was little time for play, and many children lived in such isolation that they had few if any playmates. Nevertheless, youngsters on the frontier also had a whole world of wonder in which to play. If they had few ready-made amusements and little planned play, they quickly became skilled at inventing their own fun, and in a world of freedom, where there were few "don'ts," they became self-reliant.

Wild creatures formed part of a child's fun. Sometimes the lonely ranch child would have a live pet, though this usually did not work out for long. Sometimes a clever boy would capture a prairie dog, but that required patience. Youngsters used to catch toads and tie a string to them. And there were prairie chickens and rabbits to chase, even if one rarely caught them by hand.

The frontier was a vast, unknown, isolated place.
Wild animals, like prairie dogs,
sometimes became pets
for ranch children.

Ranch children could have a free rodeo anytime they wandered to the corral. With calves to brand and young horses to rope, saddle, and ride for the first time, something was always going on. In spring, the work and saddle horses were usually shod, and in fall, the shoes were pulled off. With half-wild range horses, both operations provided lots of suspense as the horses snorted, reared, and kicked.

There were swimming holes and creeks to fish in. One technique for fishing without a pole was to stir up the water with your hands until the fish were scared into jumping into the frog holes in the bank. Then one simply reached into the hole and pulled out the fish, hoping all the while that there were no water moccasin snakes in there with it.

Picnics were popular. A berry-picking trip or an expedition to pick up cow chips might turn into a picnic, with a lunch of cold meat or eggs and cheese, wild berries, and the inevitable corn dodgers. Cow chip collecting prompted contests of skill to see who could throw the chips the farthest; often, they exploded on impact, to the great delight of spectators who were not standing close to the chips when they landed.

Youngsters did play some of the same games their cousins were playing back east—statue, for

Picnics were "occasions" which offered opportunities for contests, berry-picking, and pranks.

example, in which one person swings another very fast by the hand and then lets go. The one who was swung reels a few paces, then freezes into some strange position, the funnier the better. Even hide-and-seek and jump rope took on a difference when played in the great outdoors of the West.

For the days or months when weather forced children indoors there were homemade toys. Children also played cards, checkers, and dominoes. Small children played with cornhusk dolls or hand-carved toys. A popular toy was a jointed wooden bear that could, when properly handled, climb a rope.

Best of all, on long winter nights, was story-telling. This was the era of Indian battles, and during most of the years of settlement in the West, the Civil War was a very real and recent memory to people still living. Youngsters would sit on the knee of a parent or grandparent and hear tales of battles won and lost.

For those youngsters whose families lived close enough to a town, a Saturday trip there was the highlight of the week. Sometimes there were variety shows in town. For a few precious pennies, a youngster might see a sword swallower or a magician, a snake charmer or a juggler. Those same pennies might buy a peppermint or licorice stick

During cold weather, children passed the time inventing games, playing with cornhusk dolls, and making hand puppets.

*A weekly trip to town would bring contact with
the exciting world of peddlers, healers and candy stores.*

from the big glass jars in the general store, and if no
pennies were to be found, many youngsters had
fun just staring at the goods available in the store.
Then there were peddlers with patent or bottled
medicines. Their sales pitch was often as good as a
sideshow, and frequently they used magicians or

similar acts to attract a crowd to their sales talk. An amazing number of circuses traveled through the West even before the land was thoroughly settled, and famous opera stars such as Jenny Lind and actresses such as Sarah Bernhardt performed in the West.

Traveling circuses, with their collection of exotic performers, delighted children and adults alike.

*Although Christmas was a very special
holiday in the Old West, it was celebrated
much more simply than it is today.*

Holidays also broke the monotony of life on the frontier. The two big holidays in the Old West were the Fourth of July and Christmas. The former tended to be a community event, sometimes with a speaker, horse races, footraces, ball games, pie-eating contests, shooting contests, dancing, and a parade. But Christmas was the big event of the year. Even so, it was celebrated much more simply. There were no Christmas cards and rarely a store-bought gift. If a family lived near a stand of pine or cedar trees, they cut their own Christmas tree and hauled it home. There it was strung with popcorn and paper chains, and perhaps topped with a star made of wire and paper.

From holidays to ordinary everyday delights, the Old West was a place of fun and amazement. There was never any complaint of: "But there's nothing to do!"

GOOD OLD
GOLDEN RULE DAYS

In almost all communities in the Old West, there was school. Sometimes it was only a grade school, and sometimes it offered only a three-month term, but a school was generally the first thing organized by a community.

The first school was usually a simple one-room building—made of log or sod. It contained hard wooden benches for the students to sit on, a cast-iron stove for heat in the winter, and usually a large bell for the teacher to call the pupils. For drinking water, there was a bucket and dipper; for recreation, an open field; for "restrooms," the outhouse.

Students attended school only when their chores and the weather permitted. If they were needed at home for plowing or planting, that came first, which is why some areas had a short school term. Students came to school on foot, on horseback, and in wagons, carrying their slates, or small

Going to school during frontier times was
very different than it is today. Children
of all ages sat together and learned their
lessons in a one-room schoolhouse.

blackboards, and tablets and dinner pails. Students also brought books from home, whatever they had that could be used for reading lessons—dictionaries, histories, biographies, the Bible, an encyclopedia, *McGuffy's Reader* and *Webster's Speller*, if available.

The lessons in school emphasized the three Rs—reading, 'riting, 'rithmetic—with the usual addition of geography, grammar, and American history. There was a great stress on the literature of bygone days. A typical school day included the study of arithmetic, with problems done individually at a student's desk; and geography, during which students read assignments, answered questions about what they'd read, and drew maps. There was a great deal of memory work, and the teacher called students to the front of the classroom individually to recite either poetry or prose. Reading was done aloud, as was spelling, and in one-room schoolhouses, students recited by grade level. Older students were often called upon to help the younger children.

Youngsters had chores to do even at school. They had to gather wood or buffalo chips to feed the stove and heat the school, and there was usually a water pail, with a dipper, from which all students could get a drink. But they had to take

*This photograph, taken in Montana
in the 1890s, shows Miss Blanche Lamont
with her group of schoolchildren.*

Teachers on the prairie often
were not as prepared for frontier life
as their hardy students were.

turns filling the pail from the schoolhouse well. At recess, boys often played on one side of the school-house and girls on the other, a separation strictly insisted upon by some teachers. Boys played mumblety-peg, a game that involves throwing a knife into the dirt; or marbles. Sometimes they pitched horseshoes at a pipe set in the ground. Girls preferred to jump rope or play jacks. All of the youngsters played drop the handkerchief and hide-and-seek.

The teacher was generally imported from the East and often had to board with first this family and then that one. If the teacher were a man, he had a hard time gaining the respect of his students, whose life experiences—from a cross-country trip in a wagon to having to split firewood in the morning before coming to school—were hardier than his own. To maintain order and discipline among students who were often their superior in muscle, teachers relied on rawhide whips or, at least, a switch.

If the local one-room schoolhouse brought families together and formed them into a community, so, too, did the occasional community event—the social, or dance, often held at the schoolhouse. People came from miles and miles around for these affairs and often danced to the music of the fiddles all night.

For children, the community dance was also a time of mischief. Sometimes they played "the great baby switch." Parents generally parked their infant children in baskets on the edge of the dance floor, where the babies slept contentedly to the music while their parents danced the polka or the waltz or joined a square dance. Sometimes a group of youngsters would switch the babies in the baskets; sleepy parents at the end of the night rarely checked the baby and simply picked the basket up and put it in their wagon. They might be miles out on the prairie or all the way home before they discovered a baby girl in little Henry's place or a boy sleeping soundly in little Jane's basket. Frantic, they would return to the dance.

Another trick was to switch wagon wheels—rear wheels on the front, front to the back, so that the wagon went perpetually uphill. A great deal of work was required to accomplish this, and more work to correct it than a sleepy man wanted to undertake after dancing all night.

Such pranks probably caused anger and even despair at the time, but, looking back, they can be seen as part of the good times that characterized growing up in the West.

DANGER ON THE FRONTIER

A sense of danger was always there in the American West. Taught that "the only good Indian is a dead one," plains children grew up with a real terror of Indians, and it was not foolishness on their part. Indians had never been taught the white people's rules of warfare, and they often did not spare children in their attacks. For white children, there was the danger of being taken captive. Indians liked to take a white child captive and raise him or her in their tribes, sometimes as a servant, sometimes as a family member, often to replace a child who died. Boys captured and raised by Indians often remained with the Indians by choice. Youngsters learned to avoid being caught alone on the prairie or wandering too near a thicket that might shelter lurking Indians. They knew that Indians raided on moonlit nights and that it was better to let the Indians steal

Indians were a constant threat to pioneers, both on the road west and on the homestead. Outlaws often roamed the land shooting randomly.

Jesse James, pictured left, is perhaps the most famous American outlaw.

or kill livestock than risk their lives trying to save a horse or cow.

Sometimes an Indian visit to a homestead was prompted by curiosity or hunger rather than violence or vengeance, particularly after the 1870s, when many Indians were placed on reservations. They would enter a house, unannounced, perhaps lift the lid of a kettle and dip a finger in to taste the stew bubbling on the stove, or pick up an infant and examine the baby carefully but without evil intent. A housewife at this point was best advised to remain calm and cool, hide her fear, and give her uninvited guests the food and any clothing they might admire or request—even a horse, if that appeared practical.

By the 1880s, the Indian threat was less severe, but there were still outlaws to contend with. They too roamed the West from Montana to Texas, and while we tend to think of them as robbing banks and holding up stagecoaches, outlaws made life difficult for settlers in other ways. They might, for instance, ride through a settlement, shooting randomly just for the sake of doing so. Children were taught to listen for that pounding of hooves and to lie flat on the floor when they heard it. Ranchers lost cattle to rustlers, and outlaws would sometimes raid an isolated homestead in search of food, shelter, and even medical care.

Danger on the frontier did not come only from Indians and outlaws. It was a land in which extremes of weather threatened the lives of both people and livestock. In the summer, the temperatures could climb well above 100 degrees, and in the winter, a person could literally freeze to death going between the house and the barn. In order to work during a blizzard, settlers on the northern plains strung ropes from the house to the barn as a guide. The blinding snow could confuse a person so quickly that it was possible to be lost in that short distance and freeze to death.

The West was also a land of drought and rain, dust storms and grasshoppers. Tornados could whirl out of the sky—great funnel-shaped clouds that destroyed everything in their paths. Dust storms turned the air a dirty brown and covered everything with a fine layer of gritty dirt. During periods of drought, the water holes dried up and the grass burned brown. Yet there might be drought one season and rains so heavy the next that families were forced to flee to higher ground.

Grasshoppers demonstrated to settlers the accuracy of the Biblical description of a plague of locusts. They came as if a great cloud—a youngster

*Windstorms were one of the many
natural threats settlers had to contend
with. They were sudden, terrifying, and
destroyed everything in their path.*

could stand and watch them blot out the sun. Their wings made a crackling, rustling sound. Grasshoppers could destroy a family's entire crop in less time than it takes to tell the story, stripping leaves and leaving bare stalks. But they also climbed and crawled on people, ate rope, featherbeds, harnesses and anything else made of hide, and ruined water supplies when they fell into them. The settler's weapons against this plague were few: Prairie grass was wet and set afire, in the hope that the smoke

Settlers tried, often in vain, to fight grasshopper plagues by burning the land.

would turn the insects elsewhere; coal oil was poured on the ground and bran was poisoned. None of these had much effect on the grasshoppers.

Youngsters also had to learn to be wary of snakes that lurked in hollow trees or around mounds of sticks or dried plants. There were hornets to avoid and, in the Southwest, the vicious little wild pig known as the javelina. With their sharp tusks, they could literally shred anything— including an animal or a child—in minutes.

Rabies was a danger on the frontier, too, carried by coyotes, skunks, even squirrels. Just as today's children are cautioned not to pet stray animals, so the frontier child had to be careful about the wolf pup he tried to domesticate, the squirrel that dropped from a tree. A frightening number of early settlers on the frontier died of rabies.

Of all the dangers on the prairie, fire was perhaps the most feared. Sometimes it was caused by people's carelessness; more often, it was started by lightning. Like the grasshoppers, a prairie fire could be seen coming from a distance—a great huge brown cloud swelling like waves on the ocean, covering the earth and blotting out the sun. With it came the stifling acrid smell of burning grass that made eyes water and lungs work overtime to get a clear breath. When it was close upon a person, the

*Raging prairie fires, sometimes
set by lightning, were also a
danger settlers had to face.*

*Pioneers tried to fight prairie fires by
beating the flames with wet blankets.*

roar of the fire was even more terrifying than the
sight of the rolling flames. Ahead of it ran the animals of the prairie, seeking safety in a creek or
water hole. Inside a settler's home, milk pails were
covered with sheets to keep out ashes, and children
were ordered to stay inside so that no flying spark
might set their clothes afire.

Settlers had several ways of fighting prairie
fires. The most effective was to plow at least one
and preferably several "firebreaks" around the
house, burning the grass in the plowed furrows so

that the fire had nothing to feed on. Then one had to patrol these fireguards, putting out a thousand small fires caused by sparks that jumped the bare space. Wet blankets could be thrown on the fire, if water was available to soak them, and cattlemen frequently slaughtered a steer quickly, split the hide, and dragged it across the fire line.

Indians, outlaws, fire, blizzards, and tornadoes, rabid animals, and plagues of grasshoppers—there was much to fear on the frontier. But for youngsters who survived, who grew up accepting danger as part of life, the frontier provided a heritage of strength and self-confidence that was unequaled by that of any eastern or city childhood.

Those growing up in the Old West had an eternal sense of hope. Frontier lives may often have been bleak and gray, but families always expected things to get better.

Growing up on the frontier gave a youngster many other qualities valued today: It took courage, determination, ingenuity, self-reliance, and the spirit of adventure to live and survive in the vast, unknown openness. Those who grew up in the Old West long ago gave a rich inheritance of work and adventure, an inheritance that shaped the way Americans live today.

FOR FURTHER READING

Alter, Judy. *Luke and the Van Zandt County War.* Fort Worth: Texas Christian University Press, 1984.

Alter, Judy and Joyce Gibson Roach. *Texas and Christmas.* Fort Worth: Texas Christian University Press, 1982.

Farris, Frances Bramlette. "A Frontier Childhood," *From Rattlesnakes to Road Agents: Rough Times on the Frio.* C.L. Sonnichsen, ed. Fort Worth: Texas Christian University Press, 1985.

Halsell, H.H. *Cowboys and Cattleland.* Fort Worth: Texas Christian University Press, 1983.

Johnson, Dorothy. "Prairie Kid," *Indian Country.* New York: Ballantine Books, 1953.

Johnson, Dorothy. "A Time of Greatness," *The Hanging Tree.* New York: Ballantine Books, 1958.

Stegner, Wallace. "Born Square," *The Sound of Mountain Water.* New York: Doubleday, 1969.

Time-Life Books Series on The Old West:
The Pioneers by Huston Horn. Alexandria, Virginia: 1974.
The Townsmen by Keith Wheeler. Alexandria, Virginia: 1975.
The Women by Joan Swallow Reiter. Alexandria, Virginia: 1978.

Wisler, Gary. *Buffalo Moon.* New York: E.P. Dutton, 1984.

INDEX

Page numbers in *italics* refer to illustrations.